ELASTICITY

Ed Catherall

Wayland

Young Scientist

Electric Power
Solar Power
Water Power
Wind Power

Hearing
Sight
Taste and Smell
Touch

Clocks and Time
Levers and Ramps
Magnets
Wheels

Trees
The Seashore
Energy for Life
Flowering Plants

Elasticity
Friction
Gravity
Adhesion

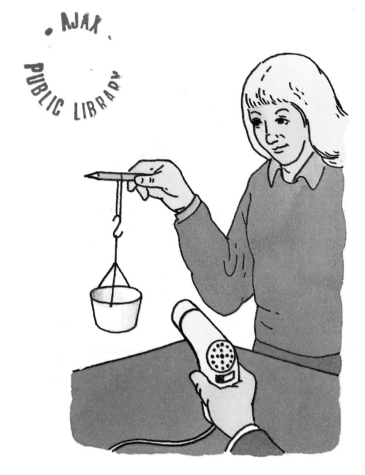

First published in 1983 by Wayland Publishers Limited
49 Lansdowne Place, Hove, East Sussex BN3 1HF, England
© Copyright 1983 Wayland Publishers Limited
ISBN 0 85078 340 2

Illustrated and designed by David Anstey
Typeset by Tunbridge Wells Typesetting Services Ltd.
Printed in Italy by G. Canale & C.S.p.A., Turin
Bound in the U.K. by Hunter & Foulis

Contents

Chapter 1 Stretching

How tall are you? 4
Stretching clay 5
Does it stretch? 6
Stretching cloth 7
Does your hair stretch? 8
Testing plastic bags 9

Chapter 2 Elastic materials

Stretching rubber 10
Is your skin elastic? 11
Bouncing balls 12
The ball and bucket game 13
Making a rubber band balance 14
Making a toy carousel 15
Making a roller 16
Rubber band motors 17
The breaking point 18
Cold rubber bands 19
Warm rubber bands 20
Loading rubber bands 21
Different surfaces 22
Surfaces in sport 23
Bouncing surfaces 24
Making sounds 25

Chapter 3 Springs

Springy materials 26
Bending wood 27
Bending metal 28
Making a spring 29
Making a spring balance 30
Making a shock absorber 31
Different kinds of springs 32

Chapter 1 Stretching

How tall are you?

Did you yawn and stretch when you woke up this morning?

Have you done any stretching and bending exercises today?

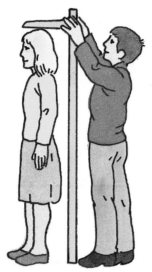

Stand against a wall.
Relax. Let your muscles go limp.
Ask a friend to measure your height while you are relaxed.

Now stretch up as tall as you can.
Be careful to keep your heels on the floor.
Ask your friend to measure your height in this stretched position.
How much taller are you?
How much have you stretched?

Measure the heights of your friends.
Can they stretch more than you?

Stand on tiptoe. Stretch an arm above your head.
How high up the wall can you reach?

Stretching clay

Roll a lump of clay between the palms of your hands to make a long clay 'sausage'.
Measure the length of your clay sausage.
Hold your clay sausage and slowly pull it.
Does the clay stretch?
What happens to the thickness of the clay sausage when you stretch it?
What happens to the clay if you keep stretching it?

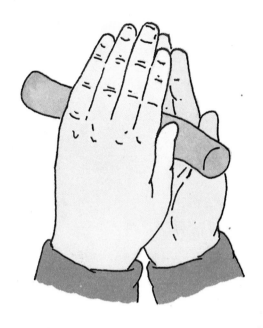

Make another clay sausage.
Bend this clay sausage.
Does the clay stay bent?

A material that does not bend easily is a *rigid* material.
A material that bends easily, but does not spring back to its original shape is a *plastic* material.
A material that bends easily and springs back to its original shape is a *flexible* material.

What kind of material is clay?

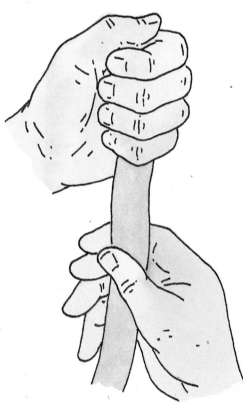

5

Does it stretch?

Find something that you think will stretch. Ask an adult if you may experiment with it.

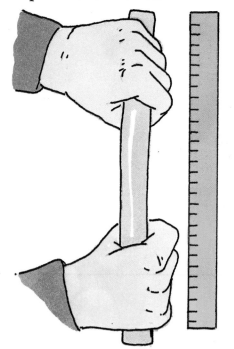

Measure the length of it.
Record its length.
Hold each end of it and pull as hard as you can.
Ask a friend to measure the length of it as you pull.
Is it stretching?

Release it.
Measure its length again.
Has it returned to its original length?
Is it permanently stretched?

What happens if you stretch it again?

Test many different materials.
Which materials stretch?
Which materials return to their original length after stretching?
Which materials remain stretched after stretching?

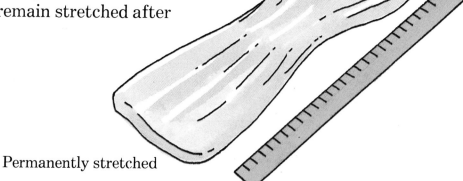

Permanently stretched

Stretching cloth

Find some different kinds of fabric.
Ask an adult if you may experiment
with your fabrics.
Sort your fabrics into knitted fabrics
and into woven cloth.

Select one piece of woven cloth.
Hold each end of the cloth and pull it
lengthwise as hard as you can.
Does the cloth stretch?
Is it easy to stretch this cloth?

Hold the cloth and pull it across its
width.
Does the cloth stretch across its width?

Hold your cloth diagonally and pull
it as hard as you can.
Does the cloth stretch diagonally?
Which way does the cloth easily stretch?

Test all of your pieces of woven cloth.
Which cloth stretches the most?

Test your knitted fabrics.
Are knitted fabrics easier to stretch
than woven fabrics?

Does your hair stretch?

Pull a hair from you head.
Use sticky tape to stick your hair to the edge of a table.
Make a hook from a paperclip.
Use sticky tape to stick the hook to the other end of your hair.

Measure the length of your hair from the edge of the table to the hook.
Record this length.
Hang a metal washer from the hook.
Measure the length of your hair.
How much has your hair stretched?

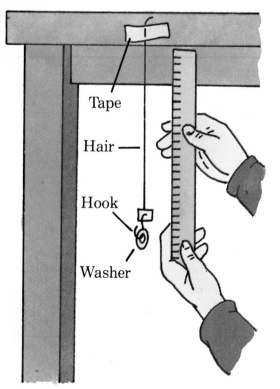

Tape

Hair —

Hook

Washer

Add another washer to the hook.
Has this extra washer made your hair stretch more?

Add washers to the hook one at a time.
Measure the length of your hair as you add each washer.
Does your hair keep stretching?
Does your hair keep stretching evenly?
How many washers are needed to break the hair?

Test some hair from different people.
Does children's hair stretch more than adult's hair?

Testing plastic bags

Use a pair of scissors to cut a strip of plastic 25 cm long and 3 cm wide from a thin plastic bag.
Use sticky tape to fasten one end of your plastic strip to a strong stick.
Wind the plastic twice around the stick.

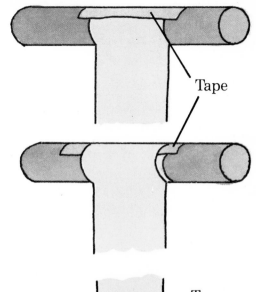

Tape

Wind the other end of your plastic strip around a pencil.
Tape the plastic strip to itself with sticky tape.

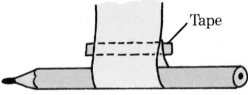

Tape

Place the stick across two chairs so that your plastic strip hangs down.
Put the handles of a small, strong plastic bag over the pencil.

Slowly pour sand or dry earth into the plastic bag.
How much does the plastic strip stretch?
How much does the plastic strip stretch before it breaks?
What happens when the plastic strip breaks?

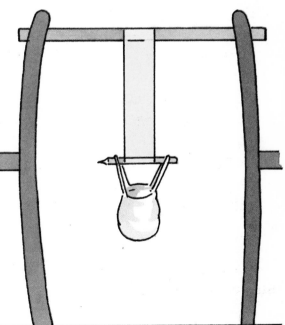

Repeat the experiment using strips cut from different plastic bags. Which strip was the strongest?

Chapter 2 Elastic materials

Stretching rubber

Use some thread to tie a large rubber band to a pencil.
Make a hook from a paperclip.
Fasten your hook to the other end of your rubber band.

Hold your pencil so that the rubber band hangs down.
Ask a friend to measure the length of the rubber band.
Record the length of the rubber band.

Place a metal washer on the hook.
Measure the rubber band and record its length.
How much has your rubber band stretched?
Remove the washer. Measure the rubber band.
Has your rubber band returned to its original length?

Repeat this experiment using two washers. How much does your rubber band stretch?
Does the rubber band return to its original length when you remove the washers?

An elastic material will stretch if a force is put on it, but will return to its original shape when that force is removed.

Is your skin elastic?

Flex the muscles in your arm.
Watch how your skin moves.
Bend your arm. Notice how your
skin stretches over your elbow.

Pinch the skin on the back of your
hand. Raise the pinched skin.
How far will your skin stretch?
Release your skin. What happens?

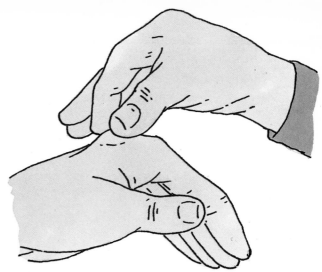

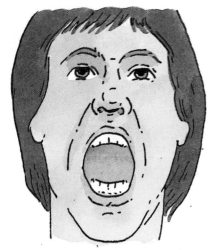

Look into a mirror. Open your
mouth wide. Notice how your skin
stretches and your face changes shape.
Close your mouth and watch the
skin on your face return to its
original shape.

Look at the palm of your hand.
Slowly make your hand into a fist.
Notice how the skin on your palm
wrinkles.

As people get older their skin
becomes less elastic.
Old people's skin is often wrinkled.
If they pinch their skin it stretches
further and takes longer to return to
its original shape.

Bouncing balls

Make a solid ball from a lump of clay.
Drop your clay ball on to flat, hard
ground.
Does your clay ball bounce?
What happens to the ball?

Make another clay ball.
Throw your clay ball hard on to flat
ground.
Now what happens to your clay ball?
What difference did throwing it make?

Find a rubber ball.
Drop your rubber ball on to flat ground.
Does your rubber ball bounce?
Throw your rubber ball hard on to flat
ground. What happens?
What difference was there in the bounce?

Watch your ball. What happens to the
ball when it strikes the ground?
Rub chalk on the ground.
Bounce the ball on the chalk.
What do you see on the ball?

Why do rubber balls and clay balls react
differently?

The ball and bucket game

Find a large bucket. Put a layer of sand or earth in the bucket to stop it from falling over.

Place your bucket on flat ground.

Stand eight paces from the bucket.

Try to bounce a rubber ball into the bucket with one bounce on the ground.

Where on the ground does the ball have to bounce to drop into the bucket?

How many times can you get the ball into the bucket in ten tries?

Which of your friends is best at this game?

Carefully watch a successful bounce.

Draw a picture to show the flight of the ball from the hand to the bucket.

Try bouncing different rubber balls into the bucket.

What do you notice?

Try this game ten paces and twelve paces from the bucket.

Does the flight of the ball change with these distances?

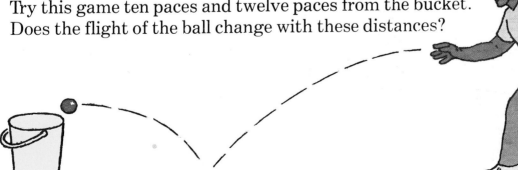

Making a rubber band balance

Find a long piece of thick cardboard.
Make a hole near to the top of your
piece of cardboard.
Push a strong rubber band through
the hole and loop it over a used
matchstick.

Make a hook and pointer from a paperclip.
Fasten the hook to the other end of
the rubber band.

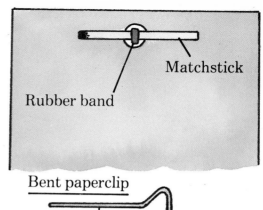

Rubber band

Matchstick

Bent paperclip

Pointer

Hook

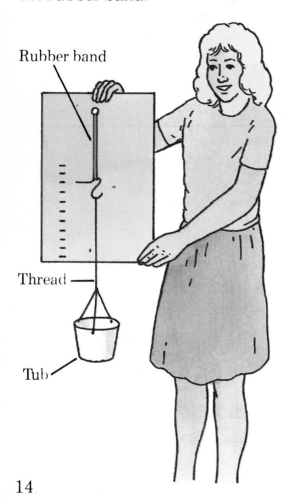

Rubber band

Thread

Tub

Make three holes around the top of a
plastic tub.
Pass thread through the holes in the
tub to make a handle.
Fasten a loop of thread to your tub
handle.
Hang this loop of thread on your hook.

Hold the cardboard upright so that
the tub hangs down.
Mark on the cardboard the position
of the pointer.
Put a weight in the tub and mark the
position of the pointer.
Put different weights in the tub so
that you can make a scale on the
cardboard. Use your rubber band
balance to weigh things.

14

Making a toy carousel

Find a cotton reel or thread spool without any cotton or thread on it.
Ask an adult to help you cut a groove across the diameter of one end of the spool.
Cut a slice from a candle.
Make a hole in the middle of the slice of candle.

Push a strong rubber band through your reel.
At the cut end of the reel, pass a small nail through the looped end of the rubber band and fit it into the groove.

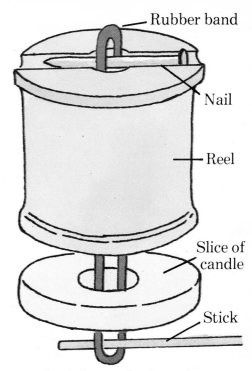

Rubber band

Nail

Reel

Slice of candle

Stick

At the other end of the reel, pass the rubber band through the slice of candle and hold it in place with a thin stick.
Draw a small plane, bird or horse on some cardboard. Cut out your drawing.
Use some thread to fasten your drawing to the end of the thin stick.

Turn the stick round several times to wind up the rubber band. Stand your carousel nail-side down.
What happens?
What happens if you wind the rubber band in the opposite direction?

Making a roller

Find a large, cylindrical can with a tightly fitting lid.
Use a nail to make two holes in the base of your can.
Make two similar holes in the lid.

Find a long, strong rubber band.
Cut your rubber band so that you have one long length of rubber.
Thread the rubber through the holes in the base of the can.
Then thread the rubber through the holes in the lid and knot the ends of the rubber together.

Pull the lid away from the can and fasten a heavy weight to the strands of rubber inside the can.
Fasten the lid to the can.

Knot

Rubber band

Weight

Roll your can forward.
What happens?
Why does the can return?

What is the longest return journey that you can make your roller travel?

Rubber band motors

Buy a plastic propeller.
Cut two equal lengths of strong wire.
Push each length of wire through a 25 cm long piece of balsawood.

Ask an adult to help you saw the end from an old ballpoint pen.
Push a short length of wire through the propeller, a bead and the end of the ballpoint pen.
Make a hook in the propeller wire just behind the pen and connect it to the wire that is through the wood.

Connect a rubber band to the hook and the back wire.
Bend the wires on top of your machine to make loops, and then hang it on a length of horizontal, taut thread.

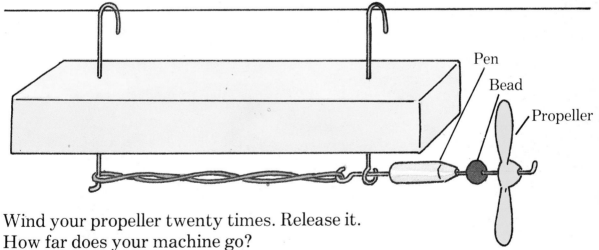

Pen
Bead
Propeller

Wind your propeller twenty times. Release it.
How far does your machine go?
Wind your propeller thirty times. Does your machine go further?

What happens if you move the back wire forward so that the rubber band is less taut?
What happens if you move the back wire back to increase the tension of the rubber band?

17

The breaking point

Loop a *thin* rubber band over a pencil.
Make an S-shaped hook from a paperclip.
Make three holes around the rim of a
large plastic tub.
Pass some thin string through the holes
to make a handle. Tie a length of string
to the handle and the hook.
Hook the tub to the rubber band.
Hold your pencil so that the tub hangs
down.

Ask a friend to measure the length of
the rubber band.
Load the tub with small weights.
*Be careful. When the rubber band breaks
the falling weights could harm you.*

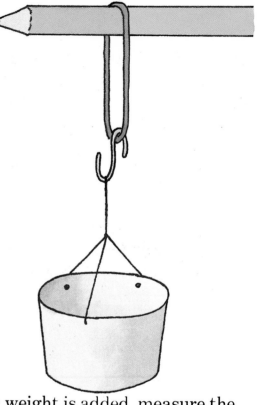

Breaking point graph

Length of rubber band

Weight

As each weight is added, measure the
length of the rubber band.
Record your results as a graph.

At which weight does your rubber band
break? This is the breaking point of the
rubber band.
Does the rubber band stretch evenly?
What happens just before your rubber
band breaks?

Does a similar rubber band break in the
same way?

Cold rubber bands

Make a breaking point apparatus
(see page 18).
Find several similar *thin* rubber
bands.
What average weight will these
rubber bands hold before breaking
(see page 18)?

Put some unused rubber bands in a
refrigerator and some in a freezer.
Leave the rubber bands until they
are cold.

Use your breaking point apparatus
to find the breaking point of your
rubber bands that have been kept in
the refrigerator.
You will have to work quickly before
the rubber bands warm up.
Does cooling rubber bands make
them easier to break?

Find the breaking point of rubber
bands that you have frozen in the
freezer.
Do frozen rubber bands break more
easily than cool rubber bands?

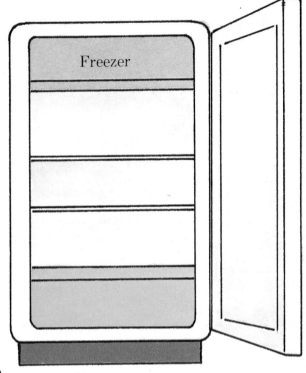

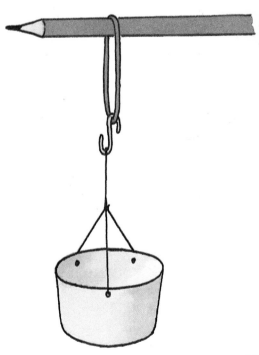

19

Warm rubber bands

Make a breaking point apparatus (see page 18).
Find several similar *thin* rubber bands.
What average weight will these rubber
bands hold before breaking (see page 18)?

On a hot sunny day let the sun warm the
rubber bands.
Do the breaking point experiment in the
sunshine.
If the sunshine is not hot enough, you
could warm the bands with warm air
from a hair dryer.

Do warm rubber bands stretch further
than cool rubber bands?
Do warm rubber bands hold more
weight before they break?

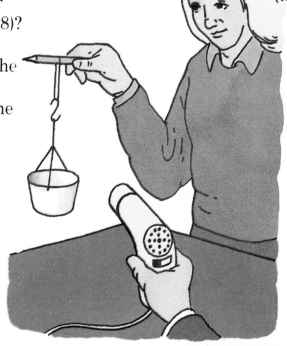

Loading rubber bands

Make a rubber band balance (see page 14).
Load the plastic tub so that the rubber band is well stretched.
Record the position of the pointer on the scale.

Hang your balance in a place where it may remain undisturbed for several days.
Make sure that the weight is constantly stretching the rubber band.
Each day look at the pointer.
Has your rubber band stretched further?
Does it keep stretching each day although you have not added more weight?

After several days remove the weight.
Does the pointer return to its original place? The rubber band has been permanently stretched.
This stretching is known as creep.

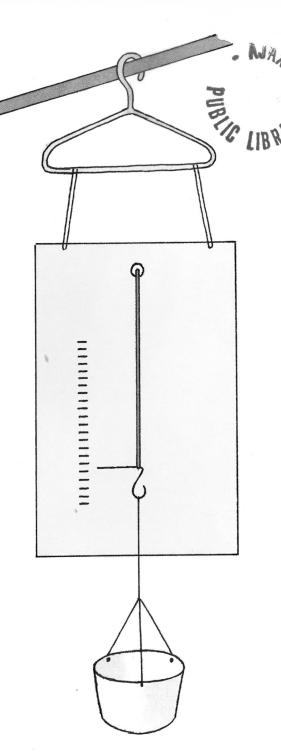

Different surfaces

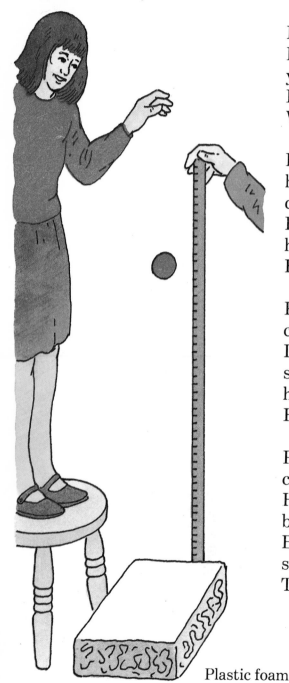

Plastic foam

Drop a stone on to soft ground.
Be careful not to drop the stone on
your feet.
Does the stone bounce?
What happens to the soft ground?

Drop a rubber ball from a measured
height on to soft ground. How high
does your rubber ball bounce?
Drop your rubber ball from the same
height on to concrete.
How high does your rubber ball bounce?

Place a sheet of plastic foam on some
concrete.
Drop your rubber ball on to the
sheet of plastic foam from a known
height.
How high does your rubber ball bounce?

Place a sheet of foam rubber on
concrete.
How high does your rubber ball
bounce on foam rubber?
Bounce your rubber ball on different
surfaces. Measure the bounce.
Try to explain your results.

Surfaces in sport

Do you play table tennis?
Look at some different table tennis bats.
What covers the surface of the bats?
How are the bat surfaces designed to
grip the ball?
On which bat surface does your table
tennis ball bounce the most?
What differences do you notice between
a cheap and an expensive bat?

Do you play tennis?
Who is the best tennis player in the world?
On which surface does this player play best?
Notice how the ball is hit in tennis.
Here strings are used to grip the ball.
What different kinds of strings can you buy?
The elasticity and the tension of the
strings controls the flight of the ball.
Which other sports use elasticity?

Bouncing surfaces

Have you ever been on a trampoline?
What makes a trampoline bounce?

Stretch a piece of rubber from a balloon
over the end of a large, empty plastic
tub.
Use a strong rubber band to hold the
rubber sheet smoothly in place.
Drop some dried peas from a measured
height on to the rubber surface.
How high do the peas bounce?

Slacken the rubber sheet.
What happens when you bounce peas on
the slack surface?

Tightly stretch the rubber sheet.
What happens when you bounce the
peas on this taut surface?
What does tension do to the bounce?

Put some dried peas or dry rice grains on
the rubber surface.
What happens when you tap the surface
with a pencil?

Making sounds

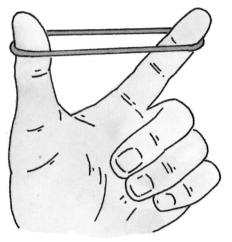

Put a rubber band over your finger and thumb.
Pluck your rubber band.
Does plucking stretch the rubber band?
What can you hear?
Can you see the rubber band vibrating?

Stretch the rubber band.
Pluck the stretched rubber band.
How is this sound different?

Put a rubber band around a large jar or an empty box.
Place a pencil under the rubber band.
Pluck the rubber band on each side of the pencil.
Are the notes the same?

Steadily move your pencil across the jar.
Pluck the rubber band on each side of the pencil.
Notice how the notes change.

Which musical instruments use vibrating strings to make sounds?
What are these strings made of?
How are these instruments tuned?

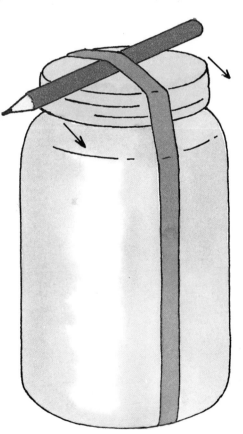

Springy materials

Place a wooden ruler on a flat table so that part of the ruler juts out over the edge of the table.
How much of your ruler juts out over the edge?
Put a book on the ruler.
Hold the book and the ruler in place and twang the ruler.
Is the ruler springy?
What can you hear?
Can you see the ruler vibrating?

Move the ruler so that more of the ruler juts out over the edge of the table.
Twang the ruler.
How is this note different?

Do this again using a plastic ruler.
Which ruler springs the most?
What difference was there in the note produced by the rulers jutting the same distance over the edge of the table?

What happens if you use a metal ruler?

Bending wood

Hammer a nail into one end of a long, thin piece of wood.
Place the wood on an old table so that the end with the nail juts out over the edge of the table.
Attach a sheet of cardboard to the back of a chair.
Hold or clamp the wood in place and mark the position of the wood on your cardboard.

Use some string to tie a bucket to the nail.
Mark the position of the wood.

Add a small, measured amount of water to the bucket.
Mark the position of the wood.
Keep adding measured amounts of water to your bucket.
Each time mark the position of your wood.
Does your wood bend evenly?

Remove the bucket. Does your wood spring back to its original position?
Pour some of the water from your bucket.
Hang the bucket on the nail.
How much water is left in the bucket?

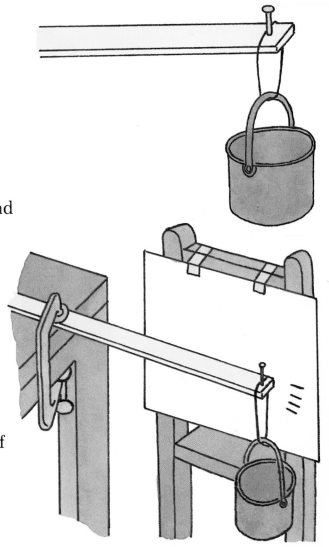

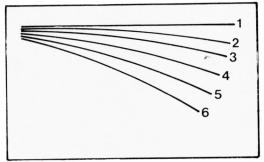

Bending metal

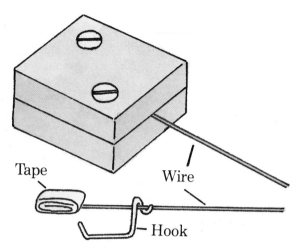

Tape

Wire

Hook

Ask an adult to find you a 30 cm length of copper wire.
A suitable diameter of wire is 18-24 standard wire gauge.
Straighten your wire.

Find two thin blocks of wood. Place one end of the wire between the wood blocks and screw the blocks together.

Make a hook from a paperclip. Wind sticky tape around the end of your copper wire to stop your hook from sliding.

Attach a sheet of cardboard to the back of a chair.
Mark the position of the wire on the cardboard.
Add a washer to the hook.
How far does the wire bend?
Mark the position of the wire.
Keep adding washers to your hook.
Each time mark the position of the wire.

If you know the weight of a washer you have made a balance.

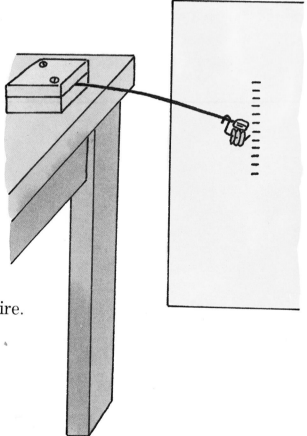

Making a spring

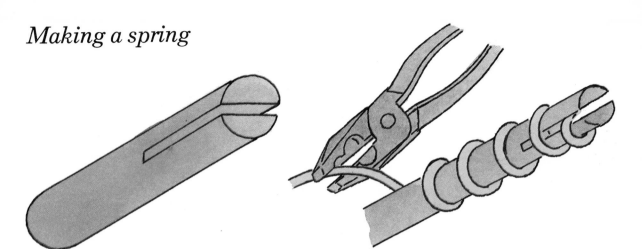

Find a short length of copper wire of 18-24 standard
wire gauge.
Find a wooden rod with a 10mm diameter.
Ask an adult to help you to saw a slit across the
diameter at one end of the wooden rod.

Clamp or firmly hold the wooden rod.
Insert the end of the wire into the slit in the rod.
Hold the wire with pliers and carefully wind the wire
around the rod.
At the end of the wire make a hook and pointer.
Use pliers to remove the wire from the slit in the wood.
You have made a spring.

Make springs of different lengths.
Make springs of different wires.

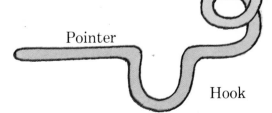

Pointer

Hook

Making a spring balance

Find a suitable spring or make a spring (see page 29).
Find a flat piece of wood.
Hammer a nail into your piece of wood.
Hang your spring from the nail.

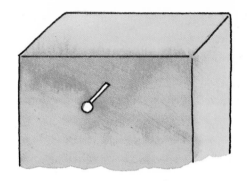

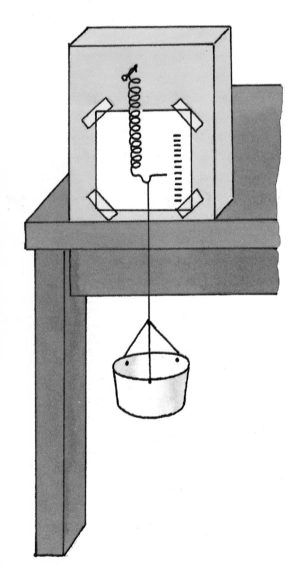

Make three holes around the top of a plastic tub.
Pass thin string through the holes to make a handle.
Tie a length of string to the handle and to the end of your spring.

Hold the wood so that the tub hangs down.
Tape a sheet of paper to the wood.
Mark the position of the end of the spring on the paper.

Put a known weight into your tub.
Mark the position of the end of the spring.
Keep adding weights to the tub.
Each time mark the position of the end of the spring.
You have made a spring balance.

Making a shock absorber

Find a large spring. Large springs are found in old sprung mattresses.
Find a can that will hold your spring.
The spring should stick out above the rim of the can.

Find another can or plastic tub that will fit over the top of the spring.
Mark the level where both cans overlap.
Press down on the top can.
Feel how it bounces and acts as a shock absorber.

Put a weight on the top can.
Mark the new level of overlap.
Keep adding weights to the top can.
Each time mark the position of the overlap.
You have made a compression balance.
Use this balance to weigh different things.

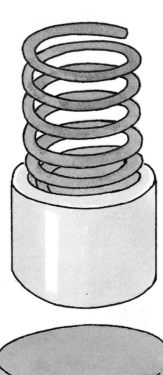

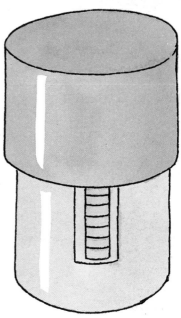

Shock absorber

31

Different kinds of springs

How many of your toys have springs in them?
Many toys are clockwork and are driven by a coiled spring.

Where are the springs in your bed?
How many springs do you think there are in your bed?
How many chairs with springs are there in your house?

Look at a bicycle. Notice that there are springs in the saddle.
These springs act as shock absorbers.
What other springs are there on the bicycle?
What are these springs used for?

There are four main kinds of springs.
Try to find places where these different kinds of springs are used.

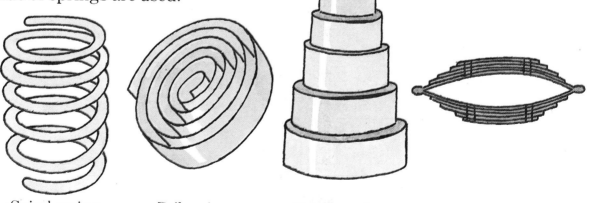

Spiral spring   Coil spring   Volute spring   Leaf spring

32